W9-AQZ-995

DATE DUE

Return Material Promptly

Everyday History

Going to School

Philip Steele

FRANKLIN WATTS

A Division of Grolier Publishing

NEW YORK • LONDON • HONG KONG • SYDNEY
DANBURY, CONNECTICUT

First published in 2000 by Franklin Watts

Copyright © Franklin Watts 1999

First American edition 2000 by
Franklin Watts/Children's Press
A Division of Grolier Publishing
90 Sherman Turnpike
Danbury, CT 06816

Library of Congress Cataloging-in-Publication Data
Steele, Philip.
  Going to School / Philip Steele
        p. cm.-- (Everyday history)
  Includes bibliographical references ( ) and index.
ISBN 0-531-14554 9 (hbk)
        0-531-15412 2 (pbk)
  1. Schools--History and criticism--Juvenile literature. 2.
Education-History--Juvenile literature I. Title. II. Series.

LA11.M33 2000
371--dc21   99-046770

GROLIER
PUBLISHING

Visit Franklin Watts/Children's Press on the Internet at:
http://publishing.grolier.com

Printed in Malaysia

Planning and production by Discovery Books Limited
Editors: Gianna Williams, Samantha Armstrong
Design: Ian Winton
Art Director: Jonathan Hair
Illustrators: Mike White, Stefan Chabluk,
Pamela Goodchild
Photographs:4 top Bill Leimbach/South American
Pictures, 4 bottom Hutchison Picture Library, 6 Ashmolean
Museum/ Bridgeman Art Library, 7 R. Sheridan/Ancient
Art & Architecture Collection, 8 top Archivo Municipal de
Historia, Barcelona/Bridgeman Art Library, 8 bottom R.
Sheridan/Ancient Art & Architecture Collection, 10 & 11
top R. Sheridan/Ancient Art & Architecture Collection, 11
bottom Bibliotheque Nationale, Paris/ Bridgeman Art
Library, 12 & 13 Mary Evans Picture Library, 14 top
National Gallery, Scotland/Bridgeman Art Library, 14
bottom Natural History Museum/ Bridgeman Art Library,
16 National Gallery/Bridgeman Art Library, 17 Dreweatt
Neate Fine Art Auctioneers/ Bridgeman Art Library, 18 top
Bridgeman Art Library, 18 bottom Discovery Picture
Library, 19 bottom Mary Evans Picture Library, 20 top
Discovery Picture Library, 20 bottom Jacob A. Riis/Hulton
Getty Picture Collection, 21 top Josef Mensing
Gallery/Bridgeman Art Library, 21 bottom Agnew & Sons,
London/Bridgeman Art Library, 23 Mary Evans Picture
Library, 24 & 25 Discovery Picture Library, 26 Bernard
Gerard/ Hutchison Picture Library, 28 Neil
McAllister/Bruce Coleman, 29 Discovery Picture Library.
Acknowledgements:Franklin Watts would like to thank
Casio Electronics and Queen's College, London for the loan
of their material.

Contents

Before Writing

I n Stone Age times, about 10,000 years ago, children didn't have to go to school. But they had a lot to learn.

This Brazilian fisherman is showing his son how to make an anchor.

Learning to Survive

They had to find out how to chip flints and turn them into tools and weapons. They had to learn how to build shelters and to hunt wild animals. They had to know which plants were useful and which were poisonous. Children knew that their lives depended on such skills.

Coming of Age

In many tribes, children were separated from their families to learn secret religious teachings. When they had passed certain tests, they became full members of the tribe and were considered to be adults. These girls are taking part in a coming-of age ceremony in Sierra Leone, Africa.

4

Important Skills

Later, people learned how to grow crops and raise animals. Children were now taught how to sow and harvest plants, herd cattle, and shear sheep for wool. Practical skills were passed down from mother and father to daughter and son. Older people in the tribe would also serve as teachers, telling tales about ancient battles or gods and goddesses.

A tribal elder passes on his wisdom by word of mouth.

Over the ages, humans discovered how to read and write and solve mathematical problems. There was more and more for children to learn about. It was time for them to go to school.

In Ancient Times

Writing began in western Asia about 5,500 years ago. The first schools were set up by the Sumerians. If you wanted to be a tax collector or work for the royal court, you had to go to school. Sumerian priests taught children writing, mathematics, astronomy, architecture, and the art of government.

Egyptian Schools

About 3,500 years ago in ancient Egypt, only the royal family and the sons of nobles and important officials went to school. The school might be a room at a royal court, or part of a temple. Lessons took place in the morning, before the day became too hot. Pupils learned how to read and write and do arithmetic. They had to copy sentences and learn lists by heart. They were beaten soundly for poor work.

Exercise Books

In ancient Egypt, broken bits of pottery were used as disposable exercise books. They also used wooden books like the one shown here. In Greece and Rome, children practiced writing on wooden blocks that were covered in wax. The words were scratched with a sharp point called a stylus. The wax could be smoothed over if you made a mistake.

Greeks and Romans

By about 600 B.C., most Greek men could read and write. In ancient Greece, boys and girls began their studies at the age of seven at private schools. Boys were taught astronomy, geometry, history, philosophy, literature, sports, and music. Girls were taught reading, writing, and arithmetic. By 300 B.C., Roman schools were modeled on the Greek system. Wealthy children were often taught at home by a slave.

▲ Roman children learned to use pen and ink as well as the stylus.

Roman children often had Greek teachers.

Monks and Scholars

Roman rule came to an end in Europe over 1,500 years ago. By then, most Europeans were Christians, and monasteries provided the main schools.

Church Schools

Poor country children had little hope of proper schooling, although some were taught to read by local priests or nuns. Larger towns had church schools. Boys of about seven to ten were taught the alphabet and singing.

▲ This picture of a monk teaching his pupils decorates a text that was handwritten about 600 years ago.

Royal Approval

Medieval Europe was a place of warfare and unrest. Many kings had received little schooling. Luckily, a few wise rulers realized the importance of education. One was Charlemagne (A.D. 742-814), who ruled most of France, Germany, and northern Italy. Though he himself had difficulty reading and writing, he founded a school and a library at the royal court and encouraged the learning of Latin.

Learning Letters

Printing was invented in China in the eighth century A.D. But there were no printed books in medieval Europe. Pupils sitting in dark libraries had to copy passages from handwritten manuscripts, letter by letter. They would try to make out the words in the Bible, which was so valuable that it was kept on a chain.

The greatest centers of learning at this time were in North Africa, Spain, and the Middle East, where Arab scholars studied astronomy, mathematics, and geography.

An Arab scholar teaches his pupils about the constellations.

The New Learning

By the 1400s, people in Europe had become more interested in learning about the world. They rediscovered the writing and art of the ancient Greeks and Romans, which seemed to have been forgotten. This new learning started in Italy and soon spread to other parts of Europe. The period became known as the Renaissance, which means "rebirth."

Students in the 1400s study law.

Merchant Schools

Most teaching in Europe was still done by priests, monks, and nuns. However, in northern Europe, many people were rebelling against Catholic teachings. They were called Protestants, and they closed down many of the old monasteries and churches. The schools attached to them often remained open, only now they were funded by rich merchants.

Apprentices

Merchants also funded the training of youngsters in practical skills, such as metalworking and weaving. The trainees, called apprentices, would leave home to learn a skill in the house of the craftsman.

An apprentice is making thimbles in this workshop.

Books for Schools

The new interest in learning happened at the same time as the arrival of printing in Europe. Printing was originally a Chinese invention, but during the 1440s, new kinds of printing presses were set up in Germany and the Netherlands. Books no longer needed to be copied by hand. They could be printed over and over again and sold cheaply. Soon, textbooks were being printed for use in school classes.

Aztecs and Incas

In the 1500s, Europeans crossed the Atlantic Ocean to conquer Central and South America. They discovered great cities and schools to match those of many European towns.

Aztec Schools

The Aztecs in Mexico had two types of schools. Noble or very clever children were sent to a boarding school called a *calmecac*. There they learned history, law, mathematics, astronomy, religious studies, reading, and writing. Girls learned weaving and embroidery.

Aztec symbols were written down on deerskin or bark.

Learning by Heart

Most children went to the local day school, or *telpochcalli*. They studied farming skills, weapons training, history, public speaking, dancing, and singing. Children learned facts by heart, singing and chanting while the teacher beat out time.

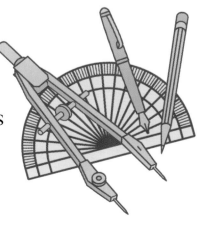

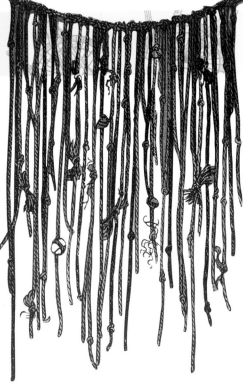

Inca Schools

The Spanish invaders found schools in Cusco, at the center of Peru's Inca empire. There was a school for noble children and the sons of chiefs who had been conquered. They learned mathematics and history, physical exercises, and the Quechua language. After four years, they took exams.

▲ The quipu was a frame of knotted cords used by the Incas for doing math or keeping records.

Harsh Punishments

Discipline was very strict in Aztec schools. Lazy boys would be pricked with cactus spines until they bled, or be made to breathe in the smoke from burning chili peppers. In Inca schools, bad behavior was punished by caning on the soles of the feet.

Breathing the smoke from burning chili peppers was an Aztec punishment.

13

Hornbooks and Quills

By the 1600s in Europe, more and more boys — but still very few girls — were going to school. At the age of six or seven, many went to small grammar school so named because the main subject was Latin grammar. Schooling lasted for about seven years.

This Dutch school, painted in 1670, was an overcrowded, uncomfortable place.

A School Day

School began at six in the morning and finished at four or five in the afternoon. Several classes could go on at once in the same room. Senior pupils helped out by teaching the youngest boys. The teacher's hand was never far from his birch cane.

Pens were cut from goose feathers using a penknife. They were dipped in inkwells.

Children learned to read and write using a hornbook. This was a wooden board with a handle. Stuck onto it was a sheet of paper covered with letters, simple spellings, or the Lord's Prayer. Children copied the words onto their slate. The paper was covered in transparent horn to protect it.

New World Schools

In the 1600s, Europeans were settling along the eastern coast of North America. The first grammar school was Boston's Latin School, which opened in 1635 in Massachusetts. America's first university, Harvard, was founded there as well, in 1636.

Make a Hornbook

1. Cut a board and handle shape from stiff cardboard.

2. Write out a list of words you find difficult to spell on a sheet of paper. Paste the list onto the cardboard.

3. Tape a sheet of clear plastic over the paper and copy the words underneath into a notebook.

Lessons at Home

In the 1600s, it was common for the father to call all the family together to study the Bible, or to teach the children about right and wrong. When the father spoke, children were expected to remain silent. They spoke only when spoken to. Both the mother and father would help their children learn to read. Older children would be tested by reading aloud to the whole family. Still, by 1700, only one in three people in Europe could read.

Governesses

In the 1700s and 1800s, rich families often paid a private teacher to visit or live in the family home. These tutors and governesses taught both girls and boys. Often the governesses were closer to the children than their own parents were.

A young governess teaches her pupil in the 1740s.

Private Lessons

Private lessons still included Latin, Greek, and arithmetic. Many children were now expected to learn French as well, which was spoken by important people all over Europe. Most children learned some history and geography. Girls would spend long hours practicing needlework, watercolor painting, music, and dancing.

Practice Makes Perfect

In the 1700s and 1800s, girls had to practice their needlework on squares of cloth called samplers. They would embroider letters of the alphabet, family names, verses of poems, words from the Bible, designs of flowers or flags, or pictures of their homes. It was difficult work. If they made a mistake, they had to unpick their stitches until they were right.

The Rich and the Ragged

At the beginning of the nineteenth century, schooling for most children was still basic or non-existent. Poor families were moving to the cities, searching for work. Their children were forced to work in mines and mills, or sweep chimneys. Some of these working children were given free lessons at "ragged" schools by volunteer teachers.

This ragged school was in the Smithfield district of London.

Boarding Schools

Even wealthy children suffered at school. During the 1820s and 1830s, many of the grammar schools became boarding schools, where pupils lived during term time. Some were good, but the worst were more like prisons.

Children were thrashed with straps and canes.

New Ideas

However, times were changing. First it was felt that the poor had the right to read the Bible. Then with the Industrial Revolution, people working in factories on complicated machinery needed to read, write, and have technical training. By 1850, half the population of Europe could read and write.

One of the first colleges for girls, Queen's College, London, founded in 1848.

Compulsory Schools

Schools were built in towns and the countrysides, and children had to go to them or break the law. Many girls' boarding schools, with women teachers, were founded. The first women were given university degrees in Oberlin, Ohio, in 1841. By the 1870s, all teachers were properly trained and children were better cared for.

Dotheboys Hall

Some of the cheaper private boarding schools were terrifying places. Young boys were bullied and beaten. They received very little food and went for long periods without seeing their families. In 1838 the English writer Charles Dickens wrote about one of these schools, called Dotheboys Hall, in his famous book *Nicholas Nickleby*.

Slates and Blackboards

Imagine you were going to school about 130 years ago. You might have to walk a long way to school, down muddy lanes. Boys wore jackets and pants, and girls wore pinafores. Poor children had ragged clothes, and some couldn't afford shoes. The start and end of lessons were marked by ringing a handbell.

An American class in the late 1890s salutes the flag.

The Classroom

The classroom was heated by a stove and lit by oil or gas lamps. Wooden desks were lined up in rows. Young children practiced writing or math on slates. The teacher, often a woman, wrote on a blackboard with chalk. Older children used lead pencils or steel-nibbed pens dipped in inkwells.

The Three Rs

Pupils spent long hours copying lessons neatly into their exercise books. Most work involved the "three Rs": reading, 'riting, and 'rithmetic. Children had to learn lists of places or dates by heart. If they behaved badly, they had to stand in the corner, wearing a paper hat marked D (for "dunce," a stupid person).

A naughty child is made to wear a dunce's cap.

In the Playground

The school yard was used for physical exercise each morning. The children did not wear special outfits. They stood in lines while the teacher made them touch their toes or stretch their arms. During their breaks from lessons, the children would play hopscotch or leapfrog, or skip with ropes.

New Frontiers

Some children in the 1800s and 1900s found themselves in wild and remote places, far from cities and schools, from the American West and the Canadian prairies, to South America, Australia, and New Zealand. Any traditional, native schools that existed were replaced with school systems of the new arrivals.

Pioneer Schools

Many pioneers took their families with them, by ship, covered wagon, or oxcart. Parents taught their children to read and write when there was time, but they were often busy clearing land and setting up the home. When an area became settled and prosperous, pioneer communities built the two most important landmarks of their towns — the church and the schoolhouse.

An American prairie school teacher calls her pupils to class.

Missionary Schools

European countries ruled lands in Africa and Asia in the 1800s and 1900s. They built European schools for the children who lived there. There were Christian missions, where local children were taught reading, writing, arithmetic, and the language of their new rulers – French, English, Dutch, or Portuguese. During the last 50 years, most of these countries have won back their freedom and, when possible, built new schools for their children.

Growing Up in the Outback

In the dry and dusty lands of Australia, known as the "outback," settlers lived on sheep stations hundreds of miles away from any others. How could children go to school? One answer was for the teacher to travel around from station to station. Another was for teachers to send lessons by mail. Some children were sent to board in town schools. Today, outback children can talk with their teachers over the radio, or use the Internet.

Between the Wars

By the 1930s, most people in Europe and North America could read and write. At this time, many people were still very poor. But children in the 1930s were better dressed and fed than in the 1890s. Many schools began to provide milk or meals.

▲ American children in the 1930s took lunch to school in a lunch box.

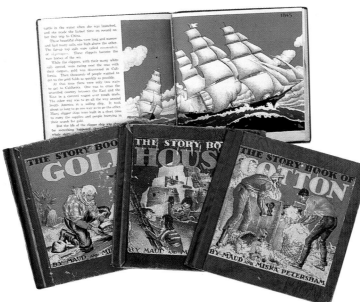

Schoolbooks were now printed in color.

Improving Standards

Children now stayed at school longer, until they were 14 or perhaps 15 years old. More were able to read and write when they left, and secondary schools often included science laboratories and halls for gymnastics. Discipline was still strict, and caning was a threat that was often carried out.

There were new charts to help children learn to read.

School Uniforms

Many schools made their pupils wear uniforms. In some schools, teachers wore a kind of uniform, too — a black gown and a tasseled cap called a mortarboard.

In many schools, the system of appointing student monitors who made sure that rules were not broken, became widespread. Other children were given special jobs to do. The ink monitor gave out dip pens to the older children and made sure that the inkwells in their desks were filled each morning.

Monitors in an American school in the 1920s check that everyone's hands are clean.

Design a School Badge

1. Draw a picture that represents your school's name or its initials, or the school's activities like books and footballs.

2. Think of a motto for your school, and write it underneath the badge.

3. Copy the badge onto cardboard and color it in the school colors.

School Can Be Fun!

In the 1950s, even young children still sat at classroom desks laid out in straight rows, and discipline was still strict.

Colorful Classrooms

During the 1960s, however, classrooms began to look brighter and more colorful. New school buildings were built with better facilities for indoor and outdoor activities. Children sat around tables and worked in small groups.

A cheerful classroom in the 1970s.

Relaxed Environment

Instead of learning lists of facts, children were encouraged to find things out for themselves. Walls were covered with pupils' projects and paintings instead of dull maps and bulletin boards. Schools became less strict. In many countries, punishments such as beating were stopped and children no longer wore uniforms.

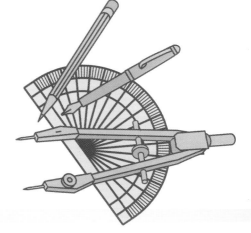

Television in Schools

Television had been tried out in schools in the United States as early as 1933. By the 1960s and 1970s, educational programs were being watched in many parts of the world.

Children from poorer backgrounds began to get the chance of a good education. In some parts of the world, like China and Russia, all children were now being educated for the first time.

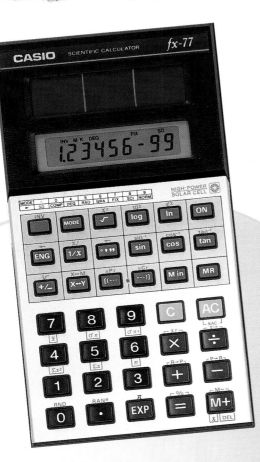

No More Math?

In 1971, pocket calculators became available. Even the hardest problems could now be solved at the press of a button. Schoolchildren were delighted. Why study arithmetic anymore? Teachers weren't so enthusiastic. Some did allow calculators into the classroom, but insisted that children still use their brains too!

A Mouse in the Class

If children from the 1400s could visit a classroom today, what would amaze them? They would see printed books on the shelves, hear lessons about space and science, see girls being treated equally with boys. They would be really astounded by computers.

Today children use sophisticated equipment to learn languages.

Computers

Computers can be used to find information, to do projects in design, to write essays and stories, and to play games. In the 1990s electronic drawing tablets were developed. These allowed the teachers to work on a diagram, as they would on a normal tablet or blackboard, but each pupil could interact with the same image on a personal computer monitor.

Information Worldwide

Today the Internet is a worldwide network of computers linked by telephone. It allows children and schools all over the world to keep in touch with each other. It gives them access to libraries, newspaper articles, and a huge variety of information sources.

The Future

In the future, will children simply use computers at home? Will teachers and classrooms exist? Let's hope so, because one important thing about learning was understood even by Stone Age hunters. Nothing can replace what we can learn from other people.

A Substitute Teacher?

Could a computer ever replace a teacher? There are already teaching programs available on computer. They can provide information, assign tasks, correct work, and give grades. Computer graphics mean that learning could become more interactive and enjoyable. But how could a computer ever motivate a student to do better, or stop a student from simply switching to an electronic game?

Time Line

B.C.

c. 3500   Sumerian schools are set up to teach writing.
c. 2520   First reference to schools in Egypt.
c. 600   Most male Greek citizens can read and write.
494   First written reference to schools in Greece.
c. 200   Education and schools encouraged in China.

A.D.

117   Roman emperor Hadrian encourages the setting up of primary schools throughout the empire.
800   The Frankish ruler Charlemagne encourages schools and learning.
1500s   Schools set up in the Aztec empire of Mexico and the Inca empire of Peru.
1540   A printed class textbook is published in England - *Lily's Latin Grammar*.
1543   First state-funded schools, in Meissen and Saxony (Germany).
1635   Latin School founded in Boston, Massachusetts.
1647   A law passed in Massachusetts requires all towns to set up schools.
1684   Teacher-training college opened in France.
1697   First Sunday schools open in Wales.
1753   First cookery lesson in school held in Scotland.
1774   Science taught for the first time in London, England.
1837   First kindergarten set up in Switzerland.
1867   U.S. Congress sets up a Bureau of Education.
1870   All children in Great Britain required to go to school until the age of 10.
1903   First schoolbus used in Paris, France.
1909   Italian Maria Montessori tries a method of replacing strict discipline with teaching that is enjoyable for children.
1924   Radio for schools set up in Great Britain.
1939–45   World War II. Education interrupted worldwide for millions of children.
1944   British school-leaving age is now 15.
1949   School television service begins in Philadelphia.
1980s   Computers in school.

Glossary

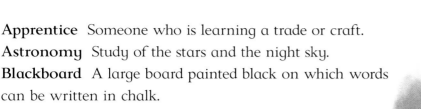

Apprentice Someone who is learning a trade or craft.

Astronomy Study of the stars and the night sky.

Blackboard A large board painted black on which words can be written in chalk.

Constellations Stars that are grouped together to make them easier to recognize.

Flint A type of hard stone.

Governess A woman paid to look after the education of children within a family.

Grammar school A type of school, originally teaching Latin and Greek grammar.

Hornbook A wooden board covered in horn, holding reading exercises.

Inkwell A small pot used to hold ink.

Manuscript A text written out by hand.

Merchant Someone who makes his or her living by trading goods.

Mortarboard A black cap worn by teachers and sometimes by students.

Quill A pen cut from the horny point of a feather.

Quipu A system of knotted cords used by the Inca people of Peru as a kind of calculator.

Renaissance The re-birth of learning and the arts in Europe during the 1400s and 1500s.

Sampler A piece of cloth used to practice needlework skills.

Slate A small piece of flat stone that was used for writing.

Stylus A tool with a sharp point, used for writing on wax.

University A place where people carry out advanced studies or research after they have left school.

Further Reading

Education: **Life in America,** 100 Years Ago series. Chelsea House, 1997.

Lee, Greg. **School.** Rourke, 1993.

Yancey, Diane. **Schools,** Overview series. Lucent Books, 1995.

Index